Ancient Greek Myths

Theseus and the Minotaur

Written by
James Ford

Illustrated by
Gary Andrews

Created and designed by
David Salariya

BOOK HOUSE

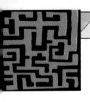

The world of Ancient Greek mythology

The Ancient Greek civilisation was one of the greatest the world has witnessed. It spanned nearly two thousand years, until it was eventually overwhelmed by the Roman Empire in the second century BC. At its height, the Greek world extended far beyond what we know as modern Greece.

We owe much to the Ancient Greeks. They were great scientists, mathematicians, dramatists and philosophers. They were also brilliant storytellers. Many of the tales they told were in the form of poetry, often thousands of lines long. The Greeks wrote poems about all kinds of human experience – love, friendship, war, revenge, history and even simple everyday activities. The most famous of the poems which have passed down to us are the epic tales of courage and warfare, where brave heroes struggle and suffer against great odds.

A map showing the Ancient Greek mainland, surrounding islands and territories

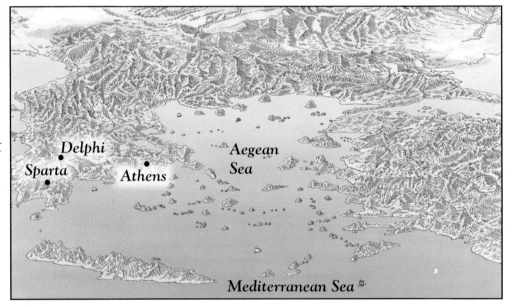

What is incredible is that until the eighth century BC, the Greeks had no recognised form of writing. All of their stories, lengthy as they were, were handed down from generation to generation by word of mouth. The people who passed on these tales were often professional storytellers, who would perform to music in town squares or public theatres. Often several versions of the same myth existed, depending on who told it and when. What follows is one version of the brave deeds of Theseus.

If you need help with any of the names, go to the pronunciation guide on page 31.

introduction

Gather round and hear my story. Settle down and listen closely, for I will tell a tale of a hero and a monster that will never be forgotten.

The island of Crete was one of the most powerful kingdoms in Greece. After old King Asterios died, people were unsure who was the rightful heir to the throne. His adopted son, Minos, desperately wanted to be King, but the people weren't convinced. So, to prove his claim, Minos promised the Cretans a miracle – he would make a bull walk out of the Mediterranean Sea.

This is an epic tale...

Minos the king

Hearing this claim, the citizens laughed and said that he was insane. Minos prayed to the god of the sea, Poseidon, for a bull to emerge from the waves. In return, he promised to sacrifice the animal in honour of the god.

At Minos's command, a crowd gathered on the beach. What happened next seems incredible. To their amazement, two huge horns broke above the waves and a magnificent white bull stepped out of the shallows. The terrified people fell to their knees and called Minos their King. However, this blessing was soon to become a curse, because Minos tried to get the better of the Gods.

A broken promise

Instead of sacrificing the beautiful animal to Poseidon, Minos kept it as a pet. In its place, he offered some of his own herd. This made the god of the sea very angry.

King Minos was the son of Zeus and a nymph called Europa. Zeus had disguised himself as a bull to attract the innocent Europa, before carrying her away across the sea.

Try this on for size.

Crete and Athens at war

King Minos of Crete and his wife Pasiphae had a son, Androgeus, whom they loved dearly. When Androgeus triumphed in an athletics competition on the mainland, he aroused a great deal of jealousy. King Aegeus of Athens had Androgeus set upon and murdered while travelling home. This provoked the anger not only of Minos, but also of the gods. Minos raised a huge fleet of ships and declared war on Athens.

Under pressure from Minos and the gods, the Athenians consulted the oracle on the island of Delphi for a solution. The priests there told the Athenians that to pay for Androgeus's death they would have to surrender to Crete and obey Minos's commands. In return Minos did not destroy Athens.

Plague!

The Gods showed their disapproval at the murder of Androgeus by sending a plague upon the Athenians. The streets became filled with dying people.

Pasiphae and the bull

Although the Gods had helped Minos in his defeat of the Athenians, the sea god Poseidon was still furious with the new king for his earlier treachery. Minos was soon to wish that he had sacrificed the divine bull. While he was away at sea, Poseidon planned to cause some mischief of his own and enlisted the help of Aphrodite, the goddess of love.

Aphrodite cast a spell over Minos's wife, Pasiphae, which made the queen fall madly in love with none other than the bull itself! Pasiphae asked for the help of Daedalus, a famous craftsman who lived on Crete. He made a cow costume for the queen, so that she could get close to the bull. Disguised in this way, she spent many happy days in the field with the sacred animal.

Ask the storyteller
Who was Daedalus?

Daedalus was a famous craftsman from Athens. When he had become jealous of his clever nephew, Talos, he murdered him by pushing him down some temple steps. Together with his son, Icarus, he had been forced to flee to Crete.

A nasty surprise

When Minos returned from Athens, he found that Pasiphae had given birth. But the child was not his. The baby was hideously deformed – with the body of a boy, but the head of a bull! This unnatural offspring was called the Minotaur.

The Labyrinth

Minos blamed Daedalus as much as anyone for this embarrassment. To cover up his shame, he ordered the craftsman to build a prison in which to lock up the Minotaur. Obeying these commands, Daedalus constructed a huge maze. This complex system of winding tunnels was called the Labyrinth and was built directly beneath Minos's palace. Once inside, no living thing would be able to find its way out and would die a slow and miserable death. The Minotaur was thrown into the dark depths of this prison, never to be seen above ground again.

Queen Pasiphae did everything she could to keep the creature from being killed. After Androgeus's death, she didn't want to lose another son. The Minotaur was very miserable in the Labyrinth. The only food he had were the rats who found their way down there. Although the Minotaur was hidden from view, he was not forgotten. King Minos had other reasons to keep the creature alive.

Worshipping the bull

Bulls were sacred creatures to the people of Crete and every year they took part in a festival where the bravest people would somersault over an enraged bull. People were often gored and killed in the process. Those who succeeded were greatly honoured.

Ask the storyteller

Did Pasiphae love her strange son?

Your mother always loves you, no matter what you look like. While the Labyrinth was being built, the Minotaur was brought up like a normal child.

A terrible price to pay

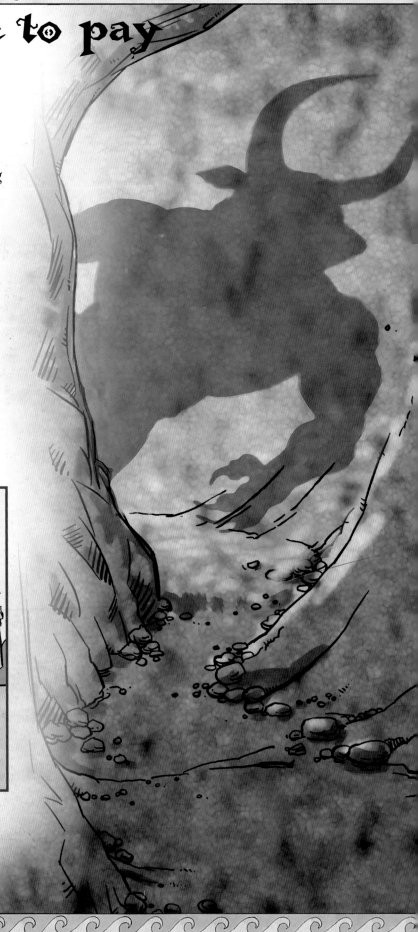

King Minos had long wanted to take revenge on the Athenians for the cruel murder of his son and now he devised a way to do so. He demanded that every nine years King Aegeus should send him a gift: seven maidens and seven young men from Athens. These poor victims would meet a terrible end in the gloomy corridors of the Labyrinth. Wandering, lost and confused in the dark, they would die in the jaws of the hungry Minotaur. King Aegeus was forced to agree to this horrific sacrifice, as the gods had commanded that he must obey King Minos.

The ship of doom

Every nine years when the sacrifice was due, King Aegeus said a tearful farewell to the victims at the harbour in Athens. They sailed away in a ship with a black sail, to symbolise their inevitable death.

Ask the storyteller

How were the victims chosen?

The victims were chosen randomly, but King Minos himself came to Athens to inspect the Minotaur's lunch. It pleased him to take this revenge for the death of his own son, Androgeus.

Aegeus's secret past

Many years previously King Aegeus had been visiting a foreign king called Pittheus. Aegeus had spent the night with the king's daughter, Aethra, and she had become pregnant with his child. Unfortunately, Aegeus was forced to return to Athens. His kingdom was being threatened in war by the Pallantids, the sons of Pallas. Aegeus hid a pair of sandals and a sword underneath a huge rock and left Aethra with a set of instructions: when the child reached manhood, he was to go to the rock and reclaim these birthrights.

Nine months later Aethra gave birth to a boy and named him Theseus. When Theseus grew up, his mother took him to the rock and he easily lifted it away. Aethra told him to go to Athens and find his father.

His father would be so proud of him!

Two fathers?

Some say that Aegeus was not the father but that Theseus was actually the son of the god Poseidon. This would certainly explain his great strength and power.

On his way to Athens, Theseus accomplished many brave deeds. By the time he reached the city, he was famous but no one knew that he was the son of King Aegeus. Theseus was invited to dinner at the palace, but the meal would nearly be his last.

Ask the storyteller

Who were the Pallantids?

Aegeus had a wicked brother called Pallas, who had 50 sons, known as the Pallantids. Pallas and Aegeus were constantly fighting for the throne of Athens.

A wicked stepmother

Medea had recently come to Athens and married King Aegeus. She was not only a cruel woman, but also very manipulative. Medea had sought refuge in Athens because she was not welcome anywhere else.

Medea was suspicious of everyone and wanted to get rid of the handsome young visitor. She persuaded Aegeus to give Theseus a cup of poisoned wine. Only as Theseus was raising it to his lips did Aegeus recognise the design on the young man's sword hilt. Just in time, he dashed the poisoned cup from his hand.

Father and son

Aegeus was overjoyed at having a son after so many years. He could not forgive Medea for nearly murdering Theseus and banished her from his kingdom forever.

Theseus sails to Crete

Theseus soon rid the Athenian kingdom of the Pallantids, but he did not have long to bask in his glory. The time had come for Athens to send its third set of victims to Crete. King Aegeus, so happy to be reunited with his long-lost son, was about to receive a shock. Theseus declared that he would take one of the places on the ship. Aegeus reluctantly allowed him to leave, but he gave Theseus a very important instruction: if he was successful he should return with a white sail flying, not the usual black one, to show that all was well. Theseus promised to remember and departed.

All was not as it seemed on the boat to Crete. Two of the young women to be sacrificed were actually soldiers in disguise. Theseus knew he would need their help in Crete. When the boat reached the island, a great crowd had gathered to greet it. Not only were the Cretans interested in seeing the fresh sacrifices, but they were also eager to set eyes on Theseus himself, who was at that time famed throughout the Greek world.

Hmmm, if those two pass for women the King must be blind!

Madly in love

Most impressed of the Cretans was King Minos's beautiful daughter, Ariadne. She fell madly in love with Theseus and promised to do everything she could to help him kill the Minotaur.

Ask the storyteller

How did Theseus get to Crete?

The boat carried Theseus out of Athens harbour, and south past the Cyclades islands to Minos's palace at Knossos.

Athens

Cyclades islands

Mediterranean Sea

Crete

Knossos

The death of the Minotaur

It would be a hard job to kill the Minotaur, but then Theseus would have to find his way out of the Labyrinth again. Luckily, Ariadne gave Theseus a ball of thread to tie to the gatepost of the Labyrinth. By unwinding it as he followed the complex maze of corridors and hallways, he would be able to find his way out by the same route as he entered. Under cover of darkness, he kissed Ariadne goodbye and entered the gloomy prison maze.

Theseus stumbled through the poorly-lit caverns, with only skeletons and rats to keep him company. Then, suddenly, he heard the heavy rasping breath of the Minotaur. Turning a corner they came face-to-face for the first time. The Minotaur's drooling mouth and sharp claws made Theseus's hair stand on end, but this was a fight the Minotaur wasn't expecting. His victims were normally easy prey. As the savage creature lunged forward to seize Theseus, the hero swung his heavy sword and beheaded it.

An escape route

Again, it was the ingenuity of Daedalus that came to the rescue. He gave Ariadne the thread to help Theseus find his way back out of the Labyrinth. In return for her help, Theseus promised to marry Ariadne and protect her from her father.

Ask the storyteller

What happened to the other victims?

The soldiers who had been disguised as maidens overpowered King Minos's guards and released the other prisoners.

23

The escape

When Theseus emerged from the Labyrinth triumphant, Ariadne was overjoyed. Along with the other prisoners, the couple escaped to the port. Theseus and the two soldiers drilled holes in the bottom of all the Cretan ships, before boarding their own ship bound for Athens.

When Minos realised that he had been betrayed by his own daughter and that his prisoners had escaped, he dashed to the seafront with a band of armed men. But as soon as they had raised their anchors and started rowing, their ships began to sink. The chase was in vain and all Minos could do was watch Theseus and Ariadne sail into the distance.

However, the couple were not to live happily ever after. A storm caused their ship to put to shore on the island of Dia. The next morning, Ariadne was in for a big surprise.

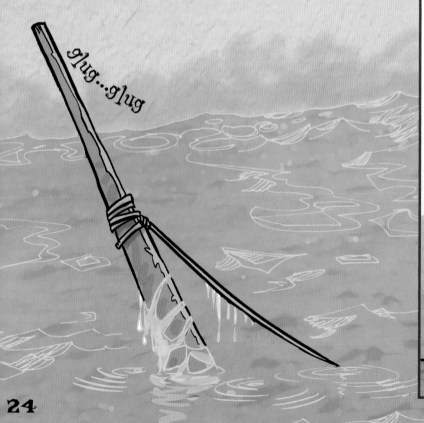

glug...glug

Deserted!

After their first night together, Ariadne awoke but Theseus was nowhere to be seen. She searched all over for him, and for the rest of the crew, but found no one. Rushing down to the shore she saw the sails of his ship in the distance and called after him.

Traitor!
I never want to see you again!

Ask the storyteller

What happened to Ariadne?

Luckily for her, Ariadne was spotted by the god of wine and merriment, Dionysus. He made Ariadne his wife and later immortalised her forever as a constellation in the heavens.

25

Daedalus and Icarus

The escape of Theseus was the last straw for King Minos. Ever since Daedalus had come to Crete, he had been nothing but trouble. Minos had him locked up at the top of a tall tower. He also imprisoned Daedalus's young son, Icarus. But as usual, Daedalus outsmarted Minos. From his cell in the tower, he lured birds to the window with breadcrumbs, before catching them. With their feathers he made himself and his son a giant pair of wings, sticking them together with the softened wax from the candles on the walls of his cell. By attaching these wings to their arms, father and son planned to fly away from Crete to safety. Though they took many months to make, Daedalus and Icarus were finally prepared. Just before they set off, the old craftsman warned his son not to fly too close to the sun. Unfortunately, Icarus didn't listen.

The boy who flew too high

As Icarus soared higher and higher, the wax in his wings melted. He tumbled downwards to his death. The sea in which he landed is called the Icarian Sea after the unfortunate boy.

Ask the storyteller

What happened to Daedalus?

Icarus's father didn't realise anything was wrong until it was too late. He eventually flew to Sicily, where he lived out his days in sorrow for his dead son.

Theseus forgets again

No-one knows why Theseus left Ariadne behind. Perhaps he was thinking of another woman in Athens, or perhaps the gods played a nasty trick to make him forget her. However, Theseus himself was about to suffer for being so thoughtless.

As his boat approached Athens in triumph, he was so excited that he forgot his promise to his father. He didn't remember to hoist the white sail as a sign that he was safe. His anxious father, King Aegeus, was watching from a clifftop for his son's return. He saw the ship with black rigging coming into harbour, and believing his dear son to be dead, did not want to live any longer. Theseus waved to his father with joy, but the old man could not see him. Aegeus threw himself from the cliff to his death. The water in which he landed was named the Aegean Sea after him.

Father!

Theseus the King

Theseus was crowned King of Athens and under his rule the city grew to be the most powerful in the Greek world. Eventually however, Theseus was forced from power and died on the island of Sciros. Many years later his bones were returned to Athens and placed in a temple.

Ask the storyteller

What happened to King Minos?

After he died, Minos became one of the three immortal judges who decided whether people had been good or bad in their lives, and whether they should spend the afterlife in torment or in bliss.

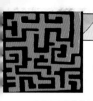

Glossary

Birthright Possessions or titles that someone has when they are born or because they are born first.

Constellation A group of stars that shows an image in the night sky.

Heir A person who will gain someone's possessions and titles when that person dies.

Inevitable When something cannot be stopped from happening.

Ingenuity Having good ideas.

Immortal A being who cannot die, such as a god.

Manipulative Trying to make others do what you want them to do.

Oracle A place where one goes to hear a prophecy.

Plague A curse of misfortune or disease sent by the gods.

Prophecy A story about what will happen in the future.

Refuge A place of safety.

Sacred When something is respected because it is holy and comes from the gods.

Sacrifice A person or animal that is killed and offered to the gods.

Somersault A forward roll in which the body and legs turn over the head.

Who's who

Aeetes (a-EE-teez) Father of Medea.

Aegeus (a-JEE-us) King of Athens.

Aethra (EE-thra) Mother of Theseus.

Androgeus (an-dro-JEE-us) Son of Minos and Pasiphae.

Aphrodite (aff-ro-DY-tee) Goddess of love.

Apollo (a-POLL-oh) God of medicine and music.

Ariadne (a-ree-AD-nee) Daughter of Minos.

Asterios (ass-TE-ree-oss) King of Crete.

Daedalus (DED-a-luss) Athenian craftsman and father of Icarus.

Dionysus (dee-on-EE-suss) God of wine and merriment.

Europa (you-ROPE-a) Mother of Minos.

Icarus (IK-a-russ) Son of Daedalus.

Jason (JAY-sun) A hero who was married to Medea.

Medea (med-EE-a) Wife of Aegeus, who was previously married to Jason.

Minos (MINE-oss) King of Crete.

Minotaur (MINE-uh-tor) Half-bull, half-human son of Pasiphae and a sacred bull.

Pallas (PAL-us) Brother of Aegeus.

Pasiphae (PASS-if-ee) Wife of Minos and mother of Androgeus.

Poseidon (poss-EYE-don) God of the sea and brother of Zeus.

Talos (TAL-us) Murdered nephew of Daedalus.

Theseus (THEE-see-us) Son of King Aegeus and Aethra.

Zeus (ZYOOS) King of all the gods and brother of Poseidon.

Index